MOVING TO SAN FRANCISCO

A GUIDE FOR N

By
Kieran Green

Published by
BookSumo, a division of Saxonberg Associates
http://www.booksumo.com/

Let's Be Friends :)

I adore my readers and love connecting with them socially. Please follow the links below so we can connect on Facebook, Twitter, and Google+.

Facebook

Twitter

Google +

I also have a blog that I regularly update for my readers so check it out below.

My Blog

INTRODUCTION
WHY SAN FRANCISCO?

First, I would like to thank you for taking the time to purchase my book, *Moving to San Francisco: A Guide For Non-Tourists*. I hope this book reaches you in the best of health and the best of times.

It was my intention in writing this book to compile a succinct guide for those individuals who are either in the process of moving to San Francisco, California or those who are considering a move. If you are a part of the group of people moving here; then congratulations because you made the right choice by selecting San Francisco as your new home. But if you are only considering your options and San Francisco, CA is one of them, then please stop deliberating and make the move!

Known for its cool summers, steep hills, beautiful landmarks, and tech giants, San Francisco is a great place filled with great welcoming people.

In *Moving to San Francisco: A Guide For Non-Tourists* you will find everything you need to know about San Francisco, California. This book will take you from a complete tourist to a local in no time.

This book will talk about topics ranging from educational options to shopping centres. We touch upon all the important details that you need to know to make your transition into this city easy; for example, we discuss the following topics: public transportation costs, rental rates, neighbourhood choices, and much more!

So without further ado let us move on to the table of contents to outline what topics are covered in this moving guide and then finally on to the meat and potatoes of the book, beginning with a short and sweet history of your new home: San Francisco, California!

TABLE OF CONTENTS

Notice to Print Readers:

Hey, because you purchased the print version of this book you are entitled to its original digital version for free by Amazon.

So when you have the time, please review your purchases, and download the Kindle version of this book.

You might enjoy consuming this book more in its original digital format.

;)

But, in any case, take care and enjoy reading in whatever format you choose!

Legal Notes

CHAPTER 1
BRIEF HISTORY OF SAN FRANCISCO

Before you become a full-blooded San Franciscan, you should know how the city has become one of the most vibrant in the United States. Let me give you a brief introduction on the events that led to San Francisco's development from being an untouched natural harbour to being the home of military power and technology.

THE EARLY SAN FRANCISCANS

The story of the city begins with the settlement of its first inhabitants. Around 3000 B.C., the Ohlone-speaking Yelamu tribe or simply known as the Ohlone people, arrived at the coast of California from parts of Europe. Their civilization rose with the establishment of chiefdoms. However, this form of government also brought instability to the tribe's way of living. Nevertheless, they remained as residents in the territory until the Spanish takeover in 1776. Today, remnants of the civilization are preserved in the Bay Area such as "shellmounds".

The period of exploration was also the time wherein the bay area was discovered. In 1769, an expedition led by Gaspar de Portola under the Spanish crown increased the influx of people in the land. However, the developments came at the expense of the colonization of the current residents, primarily by the Ohlone people. This tribe was forced into slavery and

was instilled with Catholicism. Not long after, more people recognized San Francisco's abundant resources by utilizing its hills for agriculture.
In 1821, San Francisco gained its independence from Spain as an effect of the California Republic.

THE GROWING SAN FRANCISCO: THE UPS AND DOWNS OF DEVELOPMENT

Interestingly, San Francisco was previously called Yerba Buena. In fact, it still retained the named even when it was officially named as a part of the United States. The changing of its name was only a sign of its potential to be one of the wealthiest in the country after the "gold fever".

San Francisco was not only a land for grazing and planting. Beneath its steep hills and lovely valleys was a very scarce resource: gold. The gold rush, which everyone calls it, gave a bright future to the San Franciscan economy. Samuel Brannan, the founder of the former Yerba Buena, publicized the discovery across the country; leading to a greater influx of people finding fortune.

In just one year, the population boomed from 1,000 to 25,000. This seems to be unbelievable, right? The sudden rise in the number of people in the city also resulted in disorder. The city was infested with gambling and prostitution. Even worse, series of fires caused San Francisco's instability.

However, these difficulties never hindered the city's plans for improvement. The construction of the

Central Pacific Railroad in 1859 paved the way for Chinese workers to provide labour in the city's industries. These Chinese nationals are also the earliest people to compose San Francisco's current Chinatowns.

Cable cars were also created to provide transportation with the city's steep hills. These cable cars remain to be one of the main modes of transport in present-day San Francisco.

The various faces of famine in the early 1900s still did not hinder the city's momentum. Despite the destructive 7.6 magnitude earthquake in that year which left thousands of people homeless or dead, San Francisco remained firm in developing. It hosted the Panama International Exposition after 9 years and constructed the world-renowned Golden Gate and San Francisco Bay Bridges in 1930.

Indeed, the development of San Francisco in these times could not be stopped by any hindrance.

SAN FRANCISCO IN THE TIMES OF WAR

You may be curious about the city's status when war broke out. I tell you that even in the worst wars in human history; San Francisco remained to be an economic asset for the United States of America.

As a result of US participation in the Second World War, San Francisco was the main producer of artillery for the US troops because of its strategic location and economic abundance. Being a natural harbour, the transport of arms was more efficient because it was done through water.

After the war, San Francisco was home to the conference that transitioned to the Cold War. In this city, the United Nations Charter was drafted to develop technologies that would create nuclear weapons.

THE PERIOD OF COUNTERCULTURE

If you are familiar with the hippies and active rallies, you may also know the period of counterculture. San Francisco was the haven of this momentous event in US history.

In the 1950s, the city was the birthplace of the incredible works of great writers such as Mark Twain and Jack London. Poems and other literary works enriched the lifestyles surrounded by great economics and business.

In 1967, the hippie counterculture reached its peak with the "Summer of Love", a movement bringing all hippies together in the neighbourhood of Haight-Ashbury.

Activism also joined the existing movements. Various groups fighting for diverse interests such as gay rights, environmentalism, and labor reform were a common sight in the city's districts. San Francisco retained its liberal reputation 'til now, being known as a welcoming home to LGBTQIA (Lesbian, Gay,

Bisexual, Transgendered, Questioning, Intersex, Asexual) individuals.

Now that you understand how San Francisco has become the city that the whole world loves, you are ready to be part of the history that it will tell in the future. Remember, to keep on learning about, and loving your city. Welcome to San Francisco!

CHAPTER 2
GETTING AROUND TOWN

San Francisco, because of its industrialization brought about by the rise of technology, has become more and more compact throughout the years. Because of its structural design, it's more convenient to avail existing modes of transportation if you are new to the area. If you don't believe me, try searching for parking spaces and you'll have a hard time for sure! To help you out, here are the accustomed means to explore the city and the corresponding agencies that operate them.

WALKING

The city's major tourist destinations are just a few feet away from each other. You can immerse yourself in Chinese culture by visiting Chinatown and also see other famous attractions such as the Fisherman's Wharf and Union Square. By walking, your tour around the most popular areas will be very convenient and worthwhile.

Be sure to create an itinerary to keep track of attractions that are close to each other and balance the time of your tour. If you planned a tour but become lost, in the worst possible scenario, don't hesitate to ask the locals. They won't bite you!

BICYCLING

I'm not kidding; bicycling is a trend in SF! In fact, most people prefer buying bicycles over cars because bikes can easily pass through crowded highways and fit in the narrowest of streets. Because of the volume of bicyclists in the area, traffic rules and regulations have been created especially for these commuters. So if you'll be crossing the biggest roads in the city when working, studying, or having an outdoor adventure, get ready to become a bicyclist.

If you choose to purchase a bike, remember to always keep it secure. I recommend that you buy a lock that seals your precious bicycle every time you park. Don't worry; many parking spaces are available in different parts of the city. If you still don't have the money to buy one of your own, certain companies allow you to rent. Browse this page for more information: Best Bike Rentals and Routes.

TAXIS

The easiest sign of a busy city is the volume of cabs roaming around. San Francisco, because of its industrialization, is where these vehicles swarm. Most San Franciscans avail this mode of transportation when they travel through the area. If waiting outside is too much of a hassle, then call one to fetch you.

Match the time of your commute to the least busy hours, however, so that you won't be stuck in traffic. Contact numbers of various operators are available on this link: Taxis & Rental Cars. So if convenience is the number one thing that you consider when travelling, riding a taxi is the way to go!

PUBLIC TRANSIT

One of San Francisco's major developments is in the area of transportation. It has continually innovated its various forms of transportation like buses, and cable cars in order to serve the public. The San Francisco Municipal Railway, more popularly called "Muni", is engineered to create more accessibility to the city's tourist destinations, communities, and business districts. No matter where you are from, you can always get to your desired destination, thanks to this mode of transportation.

Since laying down the routes and stops and fares and passes could be very lengthy for this book, just click the hyperlinks for each category. These will lead you to the website of the Muni's transportation authority, SF's government arm that will aid you in your trips around the city.

As busy as it may seem at first, you will learn to love the life in the city as you marvel at its fast-paced development. Enjoy your commute!

CHAPTER 3
WHERE TO LIVE

In moving to a new location, we all have our different criteria for "the perfect home". This chapter lays down the most common criteria that a prospective San Franciscan may have in mind along with the best neighbourhoods that will satisfy them.

Let's start!

First criterion: Safety

Personally, safety is the most important criteria to look for when choosing a household. Nothing beats a peaceful night of sleeping. San Francisco has 6,642 crime incidents per 100,000 residents. This crime rate is a bit greater than the national average of 3,099. Most crimes in the city are in fact violent and property-related. So you will find the neighbourhoods with least amount of crime have a higher cost.

Top pick: Presidio
Buying a house and lot costs about $1.86 million in Presidio. If you prefer renting, you can stay in a two-bedroom residence for around $2,000 a month. Crime is very rare in this community.

Second best: Inner Sunset

Housing costs in this area are far cheaper than Presidio, at $759,000 for a house of your own. We recommend this neighbourhood for individuals who may be on budget. Rental rates for Inner Sunset are similar to Presidio.

Second Criterion: Accessibility to Necessities

You always want to be near to your needs. It would be too much of a hassle to ride a train or go through a busy street just to buy one bottle of shampoo, right?

So if you want to save on transportation and have a convenient lifestyle, here are the ideal neighbourhoods for you:

Top Pick: Lower Pacific Heights

Located in Fillmore Street, you have everything you need within a few blocks. If you don't want to cook, pizzerias are readily open. You may buy groceries at the Japantown Safeway. If you need constant medications, a hospital is also within reach: CPMC. If you have nothing to do, cinemas, coffee shops, parks, and bars could kill time and are littered throughout the streets.

Third Criterion: Family-friendliness

This section is allotted for the readers who want to establish a family in SF. As a parent, you want to raise your children in an environment full of families, right? Here are the best communities whose population will be ideal for your wife and kids.

Top Pick: Outer Sunset

Thirty percent of this community's families have children. This means that your sons and daughters won't only be playing with their tablets and cell phones, they will be out and about with friends. Apart from a great number of friends for your child, you can be assured that your children will get a quality education that is close to the household.

Most of the top-rated schools in San Francisco are located within the Outer Sunset community. To add to its outstanding environment, amenities such as parks and zoos are available for family bonding!

Second Best: Outer Richmond

As compared to Outer Sunset, Outer Richmond only has 24% of children in its households and three top schools. But this neighbourhood is still a great option.

CHAPTER 4
YOUR KIDS

If you plan on raising kids in San Francisco, don't worry. Apart from being the centre of technology, San Francisco is also famous for the quality of the education it offers. In this chapter, we will provide the top three schools for various levels of education based on the ratings of competent evaluators.

Let's proceed!

Day care/Kindergarten:

Lone Mountain Children's Center
1806 Belles Street, San Francisco, California

Why this school is great for your child:

The areas of studies in the higher levels of education such as Art, Music, and Science are introduced in a manner that is appropriate to the learning capabilities of the child. Simply said, this school aims to nurture the love for learning in your child's earliest age.

Pacific Primary School
1500 Grove Street, San Francisco, California

Why this school is great for your child:

Apart from honing your child's cognitive and creative abilities, the school focuses on enhancing the child's social skills. Pacific Primary has programs that teach children how to respond to real-life conflicts so that they are ready to face them when they mature.

The Little School
1520 Lyon Street, San Francisco, California

Why this school is great for your child:

Unlike other schools where the activities are imposed and fixed, the program of this school is based on the interests of your child. Every day, your child will be asked to choose what activities they would like to participate in. The understanding comes through the teacher's guidance which is integrated in the chosen program. Indeed, learning will be fun at The Little School and will be initiated by the pupil himself.

Elementary and Secondary Education

These ratings are based on the California Academic Performance Score. This metric method measures overall school performance and improvement.

Elementary Schools:

- Chin (John Yehall) Elementary School
    - 350 Broadway Street, San Francisco, California
- Clarendon Alternative Elementary School
    - 500 Clarendon Avenue, San Francisco, California
- Lawton Alternative Elementary School
    - 1570 31st Avenue, San Francisco, California

Middle School/ High School:

- Lowell High School
  - 1101 Eucalyptus Drive, San Francisco, California

- Asawa San Francisco School of Arts
  - 555 Portola Drive, San Francisco, California
- Balboa High School
  - 1000 Cayuga Avenue, San Francisco, California

Tertiary Education/ College

In an evaluation pioneered by QS, San Francisco has been rated as the 13th best city in the world when it comes to giving quality tertiary education. The rating is a result of a survcy conducted from local and international employers when asked which cities they want to hire graduates. Here are the four schools QS determined to be the best:

- Stanford University
  - World University Ranking: 7th
  - University Subject Ranking: 1st
- University of California, Berkeley
  - World University Ranking: 27th
  - University Subject Ranking: 3rd
- University of San Francisco
  - World University Ranking: 701st
- University of California, San Francisco
  - University Subject Ranking: 16th

You may browse the programs that these universities offer through the clicking the links to their websites. If you want more information about QS, feel free to read more here.

Chapter 5
Shopping

Apart from being the home of technology, quality education, and tourist attractions, the Shaky Town is also a great destination for shopaholics. In this chapter, we will discuss the three best shopping malls in San Francisco.

The criteria of the ratings are based on a wide array of categories like: mall size, architectural appearance, services, occupancy, stores, uniqueness, cleanliness, store quality, personal opinion, parking, and location. By rating malls based on this criteria you can be assured that your shopping experience will be the best possible.

Remember that the rating will be on a scale of 1-10 with 1 being the lowest.

Let's begin!

Westfield San Francisco Center
865 Market Street, San Francisco, California

Rating: 10/10

Why it's awesome:

The stores inside are high-end. Shop at Kenneth Cole, Aldo Shoes, or Abercombie and Fitch? This mall has them all plus more! Apart from these accustomed designer labels, the mall also has rising brands such as Bloomingdale's and Bristol farms.

Westfield is very accessible as well. It's in the downtown neighbourhood! Westfield is located at the corner of Market Street and 5th Street. It would be advisable to commute, however, since parking would be very difficult in the urban areas of SF.

The food is great! This mall caters to diverse tastes. Chinese, American, Italian, cuisine are available within the mall's premises. Thus, you have a variety of choices, wherever your taste buds may take you. To top it off, the prices of the food inside the mall fall within the usual range of mall food.

Union Square San Francisco
Post, Stockton, Geary, and Powell, San Francisco, California

Rating: 10/10

Why it's awesome:

Almost all your favourite department stores are present. Pick a name and Union Square has it. In Union Square, you'll find Macy's and Macy's Men, Saks Fifth Avenue and Saks Men, other stores such as H & M and Kenneth Cole are present as well.

Of course, the best food in SF is here too! You can always find a restaurant or diner that caters to each meal of the day. Breakfasts at Sears Fine Food is surely sumptuous, and dinner would be perfect at

Kuleto's. And don't forget about Cheesecake Factory. Eat your dessert while viewing the busy traffic of Union Square!

Parking is not a problem! While it's very difficult to park in most parts of SF, Union Square has an underground garage where you can let your car take a break.

Stonestown Galleria
3251 20th Avenue, San Francisco, California

Rating: 9/10

Why it's awesome:

Stonestown is known for its amazing atmosphere. Dramatic skylights decorate the premises of this mall, radiating a bright ambiance. The marble columns of this mall provide foundation to the centre court, and display great elegance. Finally, the abundance of lights enhance the already sunny mood of the whole mall.

Not every store is present, but the number is still fine. They may not have all the high-end shops, but they have viable alternatives such as Nordstrom, Macy's, and Border's Books.

Free Parking! This may be the single reason why Stonestown is one of the best in the Golden City. Not only is the parking free, but the parking spaces are ample! So if you really prefer driving, you can choose to do your shopping in this galleria.

There you have it, the best shopping malls in all of SF. If you have further questions, the links to the malls' websites are indicated above. Enjoy your shopping sprees, everyone!

Chapter 6
Entertainment Options

Living in a new city entails being familiar of its tourist destinations. Of course, if you really want to be a San Franciscan, you should visit all of the attractions that the city is known for. Here are just a few renowned spots that you should definitely visit.

Alcatraz

Known as one of the greatest prison's in American history Alcatraz is open to the public for special viewing. If you would like to see the home of Al Capone and other great classic criminals take a tour of Alcatraz with park rangers and have the story of this prison retold.

Golden Gate Bridge

The Golden Gate Bridge is arguably the best known relic of San Francisco's history. This 65-story historical giant is definitely the second place you should visit as someone new to the area.

Electric Tour Company

This unique company provides Segway tours through the city throughout the day. Segways are a very fun activity that many people never try. This activity is also fun for the whole family.

AT & T Park

This is the home of the San Francisco Giants Major League Baseball Team. Watch them play and cheer with your fellows every time they hit homeruns!

San Francisco Bay

Travel along the famous shores of the bay. If you are a hiker the San Francisco bay offers a good amount of hiking trails. There are also biking options as well.

After a day of marvel and satisfaction, the nightlife in SF offers you relaxation and limitless fun! Here are just a few of the city's finest bars where you can enjoy friendly hangouts or meet new people.

Rickhouse

This bar is known for its sleek interior, characterized by wood furnishes and towering liquor shelves. Its ambiance is also remarkable, with live bands performing different genres of music while the crowd listens from the second floor. The drinks are also amazing, ranging from the age-old classics to the newest offerings.

Wilson and Wilson

If you want a theme like no other, then Wilson and Wilson's detective-inspired atmosphere will tickle your imagination. It is designed with 1920's wallpaper, vintage cash registers, and classical menus.

Apart from feeling like Sherlock Holmes, you can have a great drinking experience at Wilson and Wilson through their "prix fixe", wherein their culinary approach to cocktails is displayed. The drinks are served as dishes in a restaurant. Indeed, this bar is one of a kind.

The Slanted Door

If you want a balance between cuisine and cocktails, then The Slanted Door is perfect for you. Unlike the usual bar set-up, the environment here is restaurant-oriented. Apart from the drinks, you can also savour the taste of Vietnamese food while marveling at the breathtaking views of the famous Bay Bridge.

CHAPTER 7
THE ECONOMY

This last chapter discusses working in San Francisco. It lays down the statistics and gives you the best employers in the city. So if your only doubt now is the company where you can work comfortably, I will help you remove those hesitations.

How much does an employer earn in San Francisco?

The salaries in San Francisco are 35% greater than the national average. The average salary of a worker in SF is $78,000. This is due to the city being the centre of technology with the biggest firms such as Google, Apple, and hundreds of start-ups!

What companies are the best employers?

FitBit

FitBit creates mobile applications about health. Their applications measure the number of steps you've taken or the number of hours you've slept. The perks of being part of this company include free Zumba classes, happy hours, delicious snacks, and a healthy salary.

Dolby Laboratories

You may already be familiar with the brand, Dolby. Well, it turns out that they are the market leader in noise reduction and audio compression. The best characteristic of this company is working with the entertainment industry. While the salaries are fine, the best benefit you can get is a movie night even before the film is shown on the silver screens.

DoubleDutch

Although DoubleDutch isn't much of a big name in the industry, it surely understands how to take care of its employers. This social event app gives its workers free burritos, coffee passes, stock options, and concerts. What else could you ask for, right?

Eventbrite

The famous online ticketing office has continually been successful since 2006. Because of its popularity, it has bccn tagged by the San Francisco Business Times as one of the best places to work. They provide access to a smoothie bar and a zen room plus flexible travel options.

Salesforce

In simple terms, this company is one of the most charitable of all. Each year, an employee gets 6 paid days off to volunteer in a chosen charity. Apart from that, you are given $5,000 so that you can financially help your cause as well.

So take some time to find a good employer. If your background is in technology then you will easily find a place of employment. You can also rest assured that your job will grant you a high standard of living.

Conclusion

So I hope that we have provided enough information to justify moving to San Francisco. The home of Silicon Valley and a place of great history, San Francisco is a destination for those seeking a great time, and a great place to relax. So stop waiting and make the move soon!

A GIFT FROM ME TO YOU...

Because I care about you, my readers, so much (and you read this entire book) I want to give you all my new books completely free from now on! Seriously. All I ask in exchange is that you post an honest and heartfelt review of the book after you have completed it.

To get all my new books completely free please go to this book's website and join our private mailing list for readers. You will receive an email letting you know my newest book is available and an occasional update on my whereabouts and things I think you may care about.

So join up and connect! You can join the private list on this book's webpage at the following link.

http://booksumo.com/moving-to-san-francisco/

Also don't forget to like and subscribe on the social networks. I love meeting my readers. Links to all my profiles are below so please click and connect :)

Facebook

Twitter

Google +

About The Publisher.

BookSumo specializes in providing the best books on special topics that you care about. *Moving to San Francisco: A Guide for Non-Tourists* will take you from being a complete tourist to Shaky Town local in no time.

To find out more about BookSumo and find other books we have written go to http://booksumo.com/.

Can I Ask A Favour?

If you found this book interesting, or have otherwise found any benefit in it. Then may I ask that you post a review of it on Amazon? Nothing excites me more than new reviews, especially reviews which suggest new topics for writing. I do read all reviews and I always factor feedback into my newer works.

So if you are willing to take ten minutes to write what you sincerely thought about this book then please visit our Amazon page and post your opinions.

Again thank you!

Interested in Moving to Other Cities?

Check out some of my similar works on different places like:

Austin, Texas

Moving to Austin: A Guide for Non-Tourists

Dallas, Texas

Moving to Dallas: A Guide For Non-Tourists

Houston, Texas

Moving to Houston: A Guide For Non-Tourists

Los Angeles, California

Moving to Los Angeles: A Guide for Non-Tourists